In the
Home

Ruth Thomson

Commissioned photography by
Chris Fairclough

FRANKLIN WATTS
LONDON•SYDNEY

SAFETY FIRST

First published in 2004 by
Franklin Watts
96 Leonard Street
London
EC2A 4XD

Franklin Watts Australia
45-51 Huntley Street
Alexandria
NSW 2015

ISBN: 0 7496 5470 8

A CIP catalogue record for this book is available from the British Library

Printed in Malaysia
Planning and production by Discovery Books Limited
Editor: Helena Attlee
Designer: Ian Winton
Consultants: Alison Curtis, Manager of Streetwise Safety Centre,
Bournemouth and Pete Isaacs, Fire Officer, Bournemouth (retired).

The author, packager and publisher would like to thank the following people for their
participation in this book: Caren, Peter, Matthew and Rebecca Simpson; Alison and
Alfie Curtis; Sophie and Hannah Kendall and Sharon Burns.

Contents

Party time

Today is Matthew's birthday. He is having a party to celebrate. Two of his friends are coming and so is his baby cousin, Hannah.

Mum has gone out to the shops to buy food for the party. Everyone else is busy, too. Dad is blowing up balloons and Matthew and his sister, Rebecca, are cutting out paper flags.

SAFETY FACTS

Using scissors

- Use scissors with rounded ends.
- Always sit down to cut things and cut away from you – not towards your body.
- Close scissors when you have finished using them.
- Avoid carrying scissors around. Ask a grown-up to get them for you.

Ironing

Dad irons Rebecca's jeans for the party.

'Don't come too near,' he says as Rebecca walks past. 'The iron is very hot.'

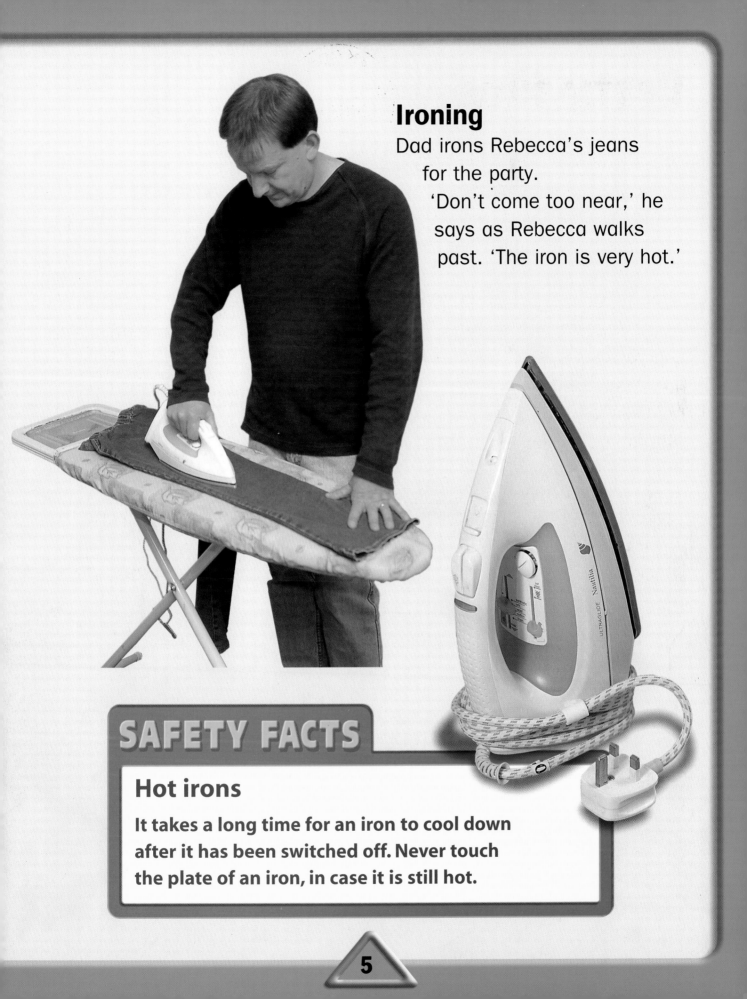

SAFETY FACTS

Hot irons

It takes a long time for an iron to cool down after it has been switched off. Never touch the plate of an iron, in case it is still hot.

In the kitchen

When Mum comes home, the children help unpack the shopping bags.

Rebecca puts the pasta and crisps in a cupboard and ice-cream in the freezer. Matthew puts the milk in the fridge.

SAFETY FACTS

Storing food

- Keep meat, fish and dairy foods wrapped and in the fridge.
- Throw away food that looks or smells mouldy.
- Keep frozen food in the freezer. Do not refreeze food once it has thawed.

Making biscuits

'Wash your hands,' say Mum, 'and then we'll make some biscuits.' Mum cuts the butter. Rebecca measures out sugar and flour. She cuts shapes in the dough and lays them on a baking tray. Mum puts the tray into the hot oven.

Washing food

Matthew washes some tomatoes and a cucumber. Vegetables and fruit should always be rinsed to wash off pesticides or germs.

Plastic bags

Mum tidies the plastic bags into a high cupboard. If a small child like Hannah pulled a bag over her head, it could stop her breathing.

Cooking

Matthew butters bread for the sandwiches. 'Why does this have a date on it?' he asks, looking at the cheese packet. 'It tells you how long it will be safe to eat, provided you've stored it properly,' replies Mum.

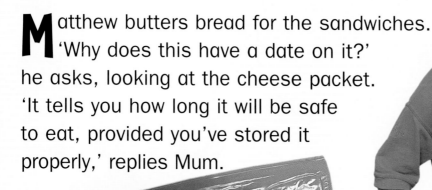

Saucepan safety

Mum melts some chocolate on the stove. She turns the saucepan handle to the side, so the pan cannot be knocked over. Suddenly the timer pings.

Hot from the oven

'The biscuits are ready,' chorus the children.
'Don't move,' says Mum, as she puts on oven
gloves to remove the hot baking tray from the oven.
'This could burn you.'

SAFETY FACTS

Cooking safety tips

• Do not stand too close to the stove
  when someone is cooking – you
  might get splashed with hot oil or
  water, or get scalded by steam.
• Keep away from a hot oven door,
  it might be very hot.
• Always use food by its *best-by* date.

A safe kitchen

When the cooking is finished, it is time to clean up.

Breakages and spillages

As Rebecca is wiping the table clean, she accidentally knocks the jug on to the floor.
It shatters with a crash and milk spills all over the floor.
'Sorry, Mum,' says Rebecca.

'Don't worry,' replies Mum, clearing up the mess. 'I never liked that jug anyway. I'll mop up the milk with an old cloth that I can throw away, and then dry the floor so that no one slips.'

All safe

Mum takes a last look around, checking the kitchen will be safe when Hannah arrives.

She pushes the toaster to the back of the counter and checks the safety catch on the cupboard where the household cleaners are kept. If Hannah tried to drink any of the cleaners, they would harm her.

SAFETY FACTS

Kitchen checklist

- Put away sharp tools.
- Keep drawers and cupboards closed.
- Make sure electric flexes do not dangle over counters.

Safe passageways

Mum looks at the bags and books lying near the front door and the shoes on the stairs.

'We'd better clear up all this clutter next,' she says. 'We don't want anyone tripping over as they arrive.'

Safe stairs

- It is never safe to leave anything on the stairs. If you tripped over something, you could have a nasty fall.
- Switch on lights in the hall and on the stairs when it gets dark, so you can see clearly where you are going.

Matthew takes his shoes and bags upstairs and puts his lunchbox in the kitchen.

Safety gates

Dad gets out the safety gates to fix at the top and bottom of the stairs. 'Once Hannah arrives, we must keep the gates closed,' he says.

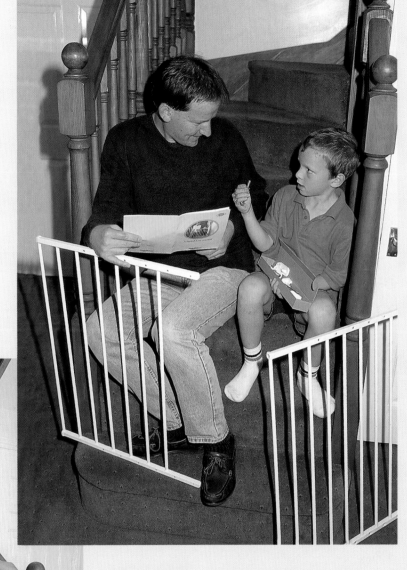

'It seems a long time since you used those for us,' laughs Matthew.
'You know how to come down the stairs safely now, holding the banisters,' Dad tells him.

In case of fire

Rebecca watches Dad change the battery in the smoke alarm. If there is a fire, this will bleep loudly to warn everyone.

Fire, fire

'What would we do if a fire started here?' she asks.
'Shout to everyone,' says Dad, 'and get out fast.'

Fire spreads quickly and the smoke contains deadly gases. 'We must keep an escape route clear at night,' Dad says, 'and think about what to do if we can't get out.'

Fire, Fire!

- If possible, shut the door of the room where the fire has started.
- Get out of the house quickly.
- Do not look for any belongings or pets.
- Call 999 from a mobile phone, the nearest house or telephone box.
- Ask for the fire brigade. Calls are free.
- Never go back into a burning building for anything.

Preventing fires

'It's best to make sure fires never start,' says Mum. 'That's why you shouldn't play with matches, nor stand or leave anything too close to fires and heaters.'

In the bedroom

Matthew goes upstairs to his bedroom with Mum. 'We'd better clear your bedroom floor next,' says Mum, 'so Hannah and your friends won't trip over here, either.'

Tiny objects

'We must put away any very small toys,' Mum continues. 'Hannah is still so young that she likes to put things into her mouth, and she might choke.'

Matthew hurriedly puts his football figures on a high shelf. Rebecca tidies her room, as well. She puts her beads and marbles in the top drawer of her cupboard.

Prevent accidents by keeping small objects like these out of young children's reach.

Safe electrical sockets

Mum checks that all empty electric sockets are covered with safety plugs. Safety plugs prevent children from poking an empty socket and getting an electric shock.

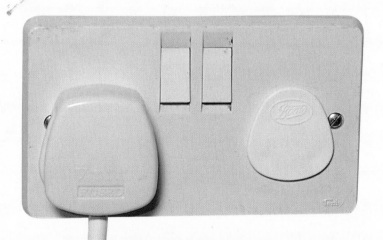

Window locks

Finally, Mum checks the locks on the windows are still secure. If the children were able to open the windows too far, they could fall out.

First aid and medicines

Mum has just started cleaning the bathroom, when Matthew comes running in.
'I've cut my finger,' he wails, holding it up for her to see. Mum quickly washes her hands and tells Matthew to rinse his finger under the running tap. She unlocks the medicine cupboard and gets out the first-aid kit.

Keep a first-aid kit. Restock it now and again, so that you always have everything you might need.

Safety pins

Sterile eye pads

Bandages

Tweezers

Scissors

Thermometer

Sterile wipes

Disposable gloves

Sterile dressings

Plasters (in different sizes)

18

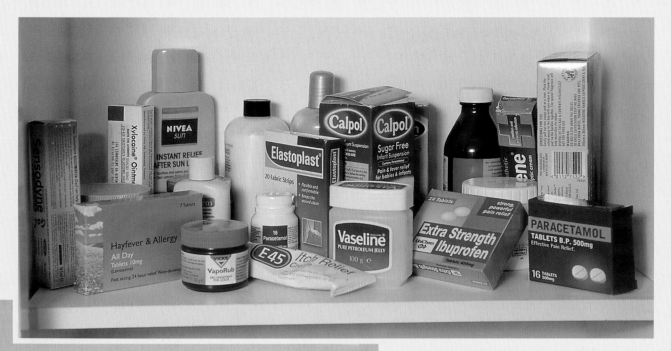

Medicines

'You must never take anything from here,' Mum says, pointing at the medicines, before she locks the cupboard again. 'These can be harmful if you take them when you don't need them.'

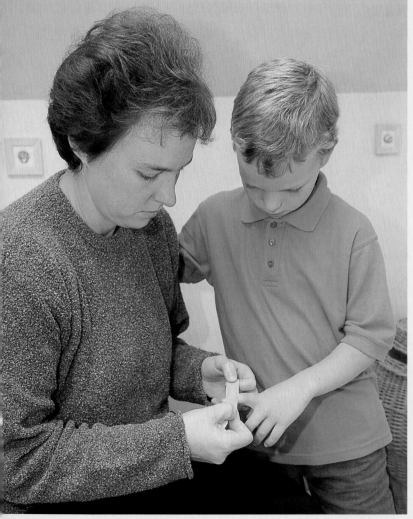

Treating a cut

Mum pats Matthew's finger dry and then she puts a plaster on it.
'All better now?' she asks.
'Yes,' smiles Matthew.

In the garden

There is still a lot to do before the party. After Dad has mown the lawn, he washes his hands and sets up the barbecue on the terrace, placing it well away from the garden fence.

He fills the barbecue with charcoal and firelighters, and lights it with an extra long match. Soon the sausages are sizzling.

If the flex of the lawn mower gets damaged, this safety plug will cut off the electricity to prevent an accident.

Garden plants and flowers

Rachel and Matthew stay out of Dad's way.
Matthew rakes up dead leaves, while Rebecca
picks a posy. She
is careful not to
scratch herself
on any of the
prickly leaves
and thorns of
the plants in
the flowerbed.

Mum uses sharp clippers to cut some
sprays of leaves with tough stalks.

Poisonous and stinging plants

'We must make sure that Hannah
doesn't try to eat any berries – some
of these are poisonous,' says Mum.

The garage

The children help Mum take the garden tools back to the garage. Mum always keeps the garage locked. It has lots of dangerous things inside it, such as carpentry tools, weed killer and other chemicals, aerosols and old pots of paint.

Storing tools

Mum carefully closes the catch on the clippers and puts them back in a box on a shelf. All the sharp tools, such as saws and drills, hang high up on hooks.

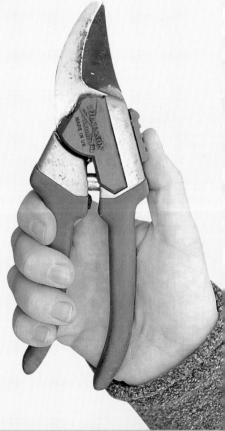

Chemicals

Many household and garden chemicals are poisonous.
They are kept on a high shelf out of the children's reach.

Warning signs

EXTREMELY
FLAMMABLE

This would be very toxic if you swallowed it or spilled it on your skin.

This causes painful burns.

This catches fire easily.

Time to eat

It is nearly time for the party. The children wash their hands again before they lay the table.
'Don't use a tablecloth, in case Hannah tries pulling herself up on it,' says Mum. 'And put out paper cups and plates, which can't break.'

Hot food

Before long, the guests arrive. The children go upstairs, while the grown-ups chat outside. When the sausages are ready, Mum calls the children downstairs for tea.

'Mind out,' says Mum, bringing in the hot sausages. Alfie and Matthew move to one side, so she can put the plate on the table.

Hot drinks

Always pour hot drinks at the table and pass them along carefully. If you passed a drink over someone's head and she moved suddenly, the cup might be knocked and spill scalding liquid over her.

Lighting candles

Mum lights the birthday candles, carefully striking the matches away from her body.
'Happy birthday!' sing Matthew's friends, before he blows out the candles.

In the sitting room

After tea, everyone goes into the sitting room to watch a video. Rebecca notices that there is something different about the room. Mum has taken the ornaments off the cupboards and the window sill and moved them to a high shelf out of Hannah's reach.

A safe fire

Mum has lit the fire to make the room warm and cosy. She has put the safety guard around the fire, to keep people away from it. If Hannah crawled near, she could not touch or fall into the fire.

Burns and scalds

If you accidentally burn or scald yourself, immediately run cold water over the burn for at least ten minutes. This cools it and lessens the pain. Do not rub butter, oil or ointment on to a burn, or touch it. Then cover the burn with a sterile dressing. You may need to go to hospital to show the burn to a doctor.

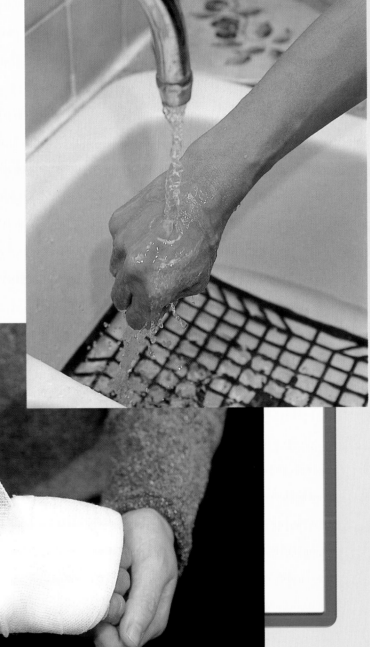

Time for bed

It is getting late by the time the guests leave. Mum goes upstairs to run the bath. She starts filling it with cold water before turning on the hot tap.

Testing the water

When the bath is full enough, Mum tests the temperature before Matthew gets in. She makes sure both taps are completely turned off.

SAFETY FACTS

A young child should never be left alone in the bath – even for a second.

Safe for the night

Dad goes round the house, making it safe for the night. He closes the windows and doors of the rooms downstairs and locks the back door. He checks that there are clear escape routes.

Switching off

He locks the front door, leaving the security chain off and the key on a nearby hook. He switches off the fire and turns off all the lights, except for the one on the landing.

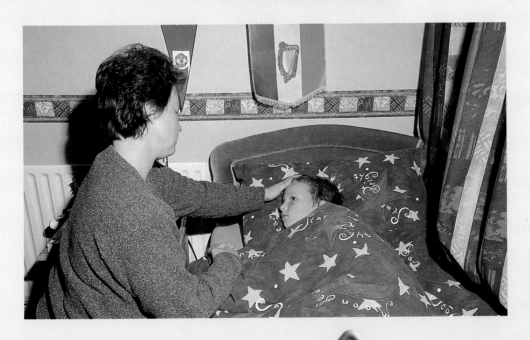

'Sleep tight,' says Mum, as Matthew snuggles down in bed.

Glossary

Burn An injury caused by touching something very hot, such as a fire or matches.

Choke When you choke, you cough and gasp because your breathing tubes are blocked and you can't breathe properly.

Dairy foods Foods made of milk, such as cheese, butter and yogurt.

Electric shock You get an electric shock when a current of electricity passes through your body. (This can seriously injure you.)

Electric socket The three holes into which an electric plug fits.

Emergency A sudden event which needs instant action.

First aid Simple treatment that you give someone who is hurt or sick.

Firelighter A white block soaked in fuel made especially for lighting fires and barbecues.

Flex The plastic-covered wire which carries electricity to electrical equipment, such as an iron, food mixer, lamp, TV or toaster.

Frozen food Food stored at a very cold temperature to make it keep for a long time.

Medicine Pills or other substances given to people to treat or prevent illnesses and diseases.

Mouldy Something, such as stale food, is mouldy when it is covered with a woolly/furry green or black growth.

Pesticides Chemicals used to kill unwanted insects.

Poisonous A poisonous substance causes illness or even death if it enters your body.

Scald A burn caused by hot liquid or steam.

Thaw When something that is frozen begins to melt.

Toxic Another word for poisonous.

Useful addresses and websites

BBC 999 programme
www.bbc.co.uk/education/999
An online first-aid course, interactive area and accidents quiz.

Child Accident Prevention Trust,
18-20 Farringdon Lane, London EC1R 3H
www.capt.org.uk
Provides downloadable factsheets on accidents to children.

Department of Health
www.doh.gov.uk
The Department of Health is active in the area of accident prevention and medicine safety.

Fire Kills
www.firekills.gov.uk
www.odpm.gov.uk
The Office of the Deputy Prime Minister has overall responsibility for Fire Safety and their Fire Kills! website contains a wealth of information and advice.

Galaxy-h
www.galaxy-h.gov.uk
The site covers a range of health topics for 7-11 year olds, using games and encouraging discussion and further activities.

Health Centre
www.healthcentre.org.uk
The web's most comprehensive and up to date index of UK health and medical internet resources.

Health Promotion England
www.hpe.org.uk/links.htm
National database from HPE provides links on health promotion related websites which often have resources available.

Home Safety Network
www.dti.gov.uk/homesafetynetwork
The Department of Trade and Industry's Home Safety Network helps to reduce the high toll of serious home accidents in the UK, and inform safety professionals and the public of the hazards.

Kid Rapt Ltd
www.childsafety.co.uk/htmlpages/safetytips.htm
A regularly updated safety tips page from a wholesale supplier of safety goods to the health, safety, and accident prevention organisations.

Kidscape
www.kidscape.org.uk
Kidscape is a registered charity that aims to keep children safe from harm or abuse. The site includes advice for young people and parents who are being bullied as well as publications and leaflets produced by the organisation.

Royal Society for the Prevention of Accidents (RoSPA),
Edgbaston Park, 353 Bristol Road, Birmingham, B5 7ST
www.rospa.com
Provides information and resources about all aspects of safety.

Safety Street,
PO Box 2078, Reading, Berkshire RG30 3FF
www.safetystreet.org.uk
An interactive safety education centre which provides safety tours covering safety in the home, in the town, by canals, quarries and railways and a building site, as well as on the road.

St John's Ambulance
www.sja.org.uk
The UK's leading first aid, care and transport charity.

Streetwise Safety Centre,
Unit 1 Roundways, Elliott Road, Bournemouth BH11 8JJ
www.streetwise.org.uk
www.homesafetygame.com
An interactive safety education centre which provides safety tours covering safety in the home, in the town and on the beach, as well as on the road. Play or download the award winning Home Safety Game free of charge.

Welltown
www.welltown.gov.uk
The Welltown website for 5-7 year olds has been designed to support safety education, set in an imaginary town. Within the site children can use the Keeping Safe in the Kitchen activity to spot potential dangers.

The Child Accident Prevention Foundation
www.kidsafe.co.au
This is a nationwide Australian charity providing advice on the prevention of accidents in the home.

The Kids Health Organisation
www.kidshealth.org
A very accessible New Zealand website with information on every aspect of child and adolescent health and safety, with quizzes, games and other activities for children and teenagers.

Index